UNDERSTANDING FAMILIES

feelings, fighting & figuring it out

by Amy Lynch

illustrated by Maike Plenzke

19 20 21 22 23 24 25 QP 10 9 8 7 6 5 4 3 2 1

Editorial Development: Therese Kauchak Maring, Michelle Nowadly Watkins
Art Direction and Design: Dan Nordskog
Illustrations: Maike Plenzke
Production: Jessica Bernard, Caryl Boyer, Kristi Lively, Jessica Rogers, Cynthia Stiles

This book is not intended to replace the advice of psychologists or other health-care professionals. It should be considered an additional resource only. Questions and concerns about mental health should always be discussed with a health-care provider.

About the Author
Amy Lynch is a writer and speaker specializing in communication between girls, young adults, and their families. She contributed to *Raising an American Girl: Parenting Advice for the Real World* and is the author of *"How Can You Say That?": What to Say to Your Daughter When One of You Just Said Something Awful*, both from American Girl Publishing. She consults about young people in the workplace through her company, Bottom Line Conversations.

Dear Reader,

This book is about you and the people you are closest to—your family. They're the sisters or brothers who bug you sometimes but who are there for you when you're in a tight spot. They're the parents who wake you in the morning and give you a hug at night. They're the people who live with you and love you, who may embarrass you once in a while, but who believe in you more than anyone else on earth.

In this book you'll find ideas and activities to help you understand your family, create memories with them, and negotiate solutions when you disagree.

Your family—with both its precious moments and its prickly ones—is your family. When all is said and done, they can't do without the ideas, the laughter, the tears, and the love that come from you. You are the girl who makes your family complete.

Your friends at American Girl

contents

family fun coupons and awards

YOUR FAMILY

Who tucked you in at night when you were little? Who remembers the first time you rode your bike or hit a softball?

YOUR FAMILY.

Your family is still here for you. And that's great—because it's easier to take the changes life throws your way when you're surrounded by people who love you. The secret is learning to understand your family and the changes they are going through, too.

family basics

There's no magic recipe for a family. Families can be made up of all kinds of ingredients. And when those ingredients are mixed together, the result is always unique.

The family in your life today might be like this:

My family recipe

- two sets of grandparents
- two parents
- my brother
- my dog, Frank

or this:

My family recipe

- my grandmother
- my parent
- my stepmom
- my brother and stepsister
- my new baby half brother

You may live with your family all in one home, or you may split your time between your parents' homes. It doesn't matter—you're all still FAMILY.

List the names of your family members here, and write one positive trait that you like about each person.

Name: _____

Something I like about this person: _____

_____

Name: _____

Something I like about this person: _____

_____

Name: _____

Something I like about this person: _____

_____

Name: _____

Something I like about this person: _____

_____

Name: _____

Something I like about this person: _____

_____

Pretend you happen to overhear your parent on the phone describing you to someone you've never met. What would she or he say? Don't think about this too hard—just jot down three or four words.

_____

_____

_____

_____

What are some good words your brother or sister would use to describe you?

_____

_____

_____

_____

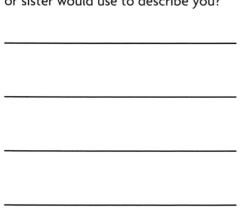

When you were younger, you would have listed different words from those you just wrote to describe yourself. Look at the words on your lists. Put an X next to words that are different from what you would have written a year ago. Those words show that *you're changing.*

BIG truth

looking back

How have you changed during the past year? Maybe you joined a team or a club, discovered you like to speak Mandarin, or learned to skateboard.

I moved last year, and that changed me. Now I know I can deal with new things, even if at first I don't like them.
—Katie, age 10

In horseback riding I can canter and jump now. Those things took courage to learn.
—Courtney, age 11

I'm at a much more advanced reading level than I was last year, and I learned to do a back walkover.
—Liana, age 9

Three things I can do now that I couldn't do a year ago:

1. _____

_____

_____

_____

2. _____

_____

_____

_____

3. _____

_____

_____

_____

green light?

By now you understand that you are changing, and fast—so fast that you're like a traffic light stuck on green for go.

This is exciting for you! But your mom or dad may act like a yellow light or even a red one, signaling for you to slow down or stop.

More than anything, your parents want to keep you safe. If you want to ride your bike to the store or go to a movie with your friends, you may think, "Fun!" But your parents may say, "I don't know about this." Then again, they may say, "Go for it!"

No matter which signal your parents give you, nothing seems the same as it was last year—or maybe even last week.

Every time you change, your family changes in some way, too. See if these examples fit your family:

• You understand jokes now, so your parents tell you more jokes.

• You are stronger, so your big sister or brother plays basketball against you more seriously.

• You are more responsible, so your family depends on you more.

• You are better at making decisions and taking care of yourself, so your parents let you make more choices.

With everybody changing and everybody busy, how will you find ways to talk about everything you need to discuss? You may wonder . . .

• where to begin if you have questions about body stuff and growing up.

• what words to use if you are sad or mad or lonely.

• how to negotiate for more independence.

Hey Mom, I have a question for you.

COMMUNICATE!

You're changing, and sometimes
changes are hard to talk about.

Now is the time to learn to communicate
better with your family—to keep your minds and
hearts open so that you can talk things out.

little things that say a lot

A loving message is like a cozy blanket or a cup of hot cocoa on a winter morning. It warms you all the way through. And you can send warm messages anytime you want.

Share YOU. Your parents miss you if you don't spend time with them. Play a game, take a walk, or bake a cake—together.

Be sympathetic. When your dad is sick or your sister gets cut from the team, let the feelings flow. Your family will feel better just knowing that you care.

Coming and going. "Have a great day" and "welcome home" can be real pick-me-ups for the person walking through the door. These may be the best words your mom will hear all day, especially since they come from you.

Give healthy hugs. People who get plenty of hugs tend to get sick less often than those who don't. So share hugs with your family and spread the good feeling around. (But remember, you always have the right to say NO to hugs and cuddles if you don't want them.)

Say "please" and "thanks." Little things count, and these little words really work. No wonder some people call them magic!

Stay in touch. When you have a good thought or a funny memory about someone in your life, text them your love—they want to hear from you!

Schedule it. Dance lessons, scouts, soccer practice, babysitting, and sleepovers—you have a million places to go. Put your schedule on the family calendar ahead of time. Be part of the plan.

how to talk to your parents about anything

Some problems are big. Sometimes you need advice. Maybe something big has happened, but when it comes to talking to a parent about it, you don't know where to start.

Maybe you're shy when it comes to talking about something personal. Maybe you're worried about how your parents will react. No matter what, these tips can help.

Plan your moment. Begin by picking the right time. You need your parent's full attention in order to have a good talk. Try not to bring up something when it's past your bedtime, when your parent is in a rush, or when she or he is concentrating on work. If it's hard to get a parent alone, make an "appointment." Your parents want to know what's on your mind, so ask them to make time for you.

Go slowly. What you need to say probably isn't simple, so don't try to get it all out in one breath. Remember that conversation is about give-and-take. Listen to your parents, and they'll listen to you.

Be honest. Your parents will respond better if they believe that you're telling the whole truth and not trying to avoid blame. Take responsibility for your part in getting into trouble or earning a bad grade. If you've done something wrong, 'fess up. Things get worse the longer you wait.

Instead of this:

But it wasn't my FAULT!

Try this:

I'm sorry this happened. I've been afraid to tell you about it, but I want to try to fix things.

Try, try again. When you fly off the handle, your parents have a hard time seeing your point of view. If you're angry or frustrated, take a break from the conversation. Excuse yourself, and go somewhere to cool off. Gather your thoughts, and when you're ready, try talking to your parents again.

Instead of this:

You don't get it! You treat me like a baby!

Try this:

This means a lot to me. I want you to understand.

Be brave. You might carry around a question or confession for a long time before you get up the nerve to let it out. But your parents almost always can help you, and you'll probably feel better afterward. Talk to your parents. You'll be glad you did.

Instead of this:

Try this:

help!

Is it hard for you to talk about your feelings? That's OK—it can be hard for anyone, but opening up with your family can make any situation better.

My parents think I need to be perfect. If I get a B instead of an A, they make a big fuss over it. It's important to get good grades, but they're overdoing it.

—Not Perfect

Parents can't help it: they want the best for their kids, and that's what makes them push. They also may focus on grades when what they really want is just to be sure you're trying your hardest. Still, most parents also know it isn't possible to be best at everything. Talk with them, and ask if together you can choose the subjects in which it's crucial for you to shine. They may be more accepting of your grades if they're sure you're reaching for the stars when it counts the most.

If my mom is having a stressful day, she can be really cranky. I hate to be around her when she's like that. Help me!

—Don't Know What to Do

When Mom has had a hard day, the best thing you can do is give her some peace and quiet. If you have siblings, invite them to play a quiet board game with you so that they stay out of Mom's hair, too. Maybe you can help out by setting the table, even without being asked to do so. Just asking if there's anything you can do for her will let her know that you're there for her. And don't forget to give her a big hug—it might be just what she needs to feel better.

My dad is really critical of me in sports. I try to do my best, but it seems like it's never enough for him. He even says rude things about my coaches.

—Discouraged and Upset

Your dad wants you to do your best. That's good. But he may have forgotten that sports should also be fun. See if you can remind him. Tell him that when he's upset with the coach or with you, the fun disappears. Let him know that cheering helps you more than criticism. Be prepared: in the heat of a game, your dad may forget to keep his cool. If so, your best defense is to stay focused on the game and your teammates—not on those shouts you hear from the sidelines.

I am a sixth-grader who got my first detention today. I feel like I'm losing my perfect reputation. I want my image and my parents' trust back.

—No Longer Perfect

It sounds as if you made a mistake. Here's a little secret—everyone does. No one is perfect, so don't be unfair to yourself by expecting to be. In time, if you show that you've learned from your mistake by not repeating it, you'll regain your parents' trust. In fact, your parents will probably forgive you more easily than you will forgive yourself. Tell them how you feel. Then serve your detention and move on!

FAMILY FIRST AID

When trouble happens (and it will!),
learn to help clear the air.

BIG truth

Families fight.
It's normal.

Your family members will not get along perfectly all the time unless they are one of the following:

• mannequins

• robots

• fairy-tale characters

If your family is made up of real live humans, then feelings will get out of control from time to time—even though you love one another with all your hearts. So what should you do when things get rough? Learn to help solve problems. If you do that, it'll be a sure sign you're growing up.

parent spotlight

Because your parents are always there, it can be easy to overlook that they are changing, too.

The truth is that parents and stepparents can't stop changing any more than you can! And the ways they change can affect your life big-time. On the one hand, if your mom starts playing volleyball, she may go to practice on Tuesday evenings instead of staying home with you to watch *Revenge of the Sharks* on the Ocean Channel. On the other hand, if your dad has started baking bread in his spare time, he may be more available for chats in the afternoon.

Explore the ways your parents or stepparents are changing by putting a check beside the things that are true.

One of my parents or stepparents . . .

☐ has found a new hobby or sport.

☐ has taken a different job.

☐ has divorced or remarried.

☐ exercises more than she or he used to.

☐ exercises less than she or he used to.

☐ has a parent who is ill or who recently died.

☐ is planning a vacation.

☐ laughs more these days.

☐ acts more serious these days.

☐ recently celebrated a big anniversary or birthday.

Do you ever get wound up and anxious thinking about your day, your homework, or problems you have with friends? That's natural.

We all get stuck in thoughts about ourselves sometimes, but when we do, it can cause family conflict . . . especially with our parents. If you forget to think about their point of view—the chores they need you to help with, the times they need you to get home, the pressures they feel to get their work done—you can get in a jam with them before you know it!

Don't stay cooped up inside your own head. Sure, it's interesting in there. But once in a while, give this mind-reading exercise a try:

1. Pick a parent.

2. Now, use your imagination. What does she or he think:
- first thing in the morning?
- when waiting at a stop sign?
- just before drifting off to sleep?

3. When you have a minute, ask your parent and find out the real answers.

See, wasn't that interesting?

stop the fight before it starts

Sometimes the people closest to our hearts are the ones we take for granted the most—and that can lead to hurt feelings and fights. Here are some ways to show your family that they matter to you.

Start the day gently. Are you half asleep in the a.m.? You're not alone. Give everybody in your family a little extra understanding in the morning. They might be sleepwalking just like you!

Lend a hand. Did you know that parents do nine or ten chores for every one chore a kid does? So clear the table, scrape the scraps, and toss the trash. You get bonus points for doing chores without being asked!

My dog is part of my family. I remember washing him when he was a puppy. I took him in the shower and then wrapped him in a towel. It makes me feel good to help out around the house. I know my mom depends on me.
—Hannah, age 10

Notice your noise. Music is great! But don't play it too loud. Use headphones or turn down the volume when your brother is doing his homework or your mom is taking a nap. It's better for your eardrums, too.

Try to do your homework early. The closer it is to bedtime, the harder it is to get the work done, and the harder it is for your parents to help.

Stash your stuff. Keeping your things in your room helps the family stay on the go. And nobody will trip over your backpack in the hallway.

Beat a retreat. Feeling moody? Try not to take it out on your family. When you know you're crabby, do something that soothes you, like playing with your pet, taking a warm bath, or reading a good book.

Not now, but later. When you ask someone in the family for help or for a favor, try asking for it later instead of right this minute. Then the answer is more likely to be yes.

Joke gently. Some people in your family probably can make a joke and take a joke, but not everyone can. And even those who can, can't take jokes all the time. Respect the feelings family members have about teasing and tickling. They'll be more likely to respect your feelings, too.

BIG truth

your reaction style

When there is conflict at home, how do you react? Think about the last time you got into an argument with a member of your family. Below, choose the kind of geography that best describes the way you reacted to the situation.

☐ **Volcano:** You exploded with a flash of flame. Then your anger went away pretty quickly.

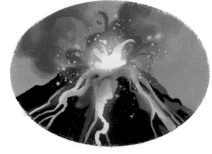

☐ **Iceberg:** You didn't go on the attack, but you had lots of angry feelings underneath the surface. Those feelings lasted a long time after the fight was over.

☐ **Rock:** During the argument, your thoughts and reactions slowed down and felt heavy, like boulders. It was hard to find the words you wanted.

☐ **River:** Your mind was working at top speed. You thought of lots of ways to make others see things your way, and the words came easily to you.

Each reaction style has the power to do harm. A volcano makes everybody cower. An iceberg remembers hurts. A rock resists solutions, and a river is determined to make other people agree with her.

Now, here's the best part. You can use the power of your reaction style for making up!

Volcano: Your flash of flaming anger may have inflicted more hurt than you realize, and there's nothing like a sincere apology for making things right. In fact, apologize twice. Over time you'll learn to cool the flames with people you love.

Iceberg: Wait a day before you make your next move. Then check in with the family member who argued with you. Tell him or her that you are trying to let go of hard feelings. Offer a hug if you are ready, and feel the world of love inside the hug that you get.

Rock: People may think you aren't upset by the fight or that you don't care about their hurt feelings. No matter what your part was in the argument, be sure to tell the other person that you know she is upset and that you care about how she feels. Then she'll know how strong and true your heart is!

River: Remember that there is no "right" in a fight. You may win the argument but leave lots of hard feelings behind. Next time, do something radical—practice losing! That's right; let somebody else have the last word and see what happens. Peace can return more quickly that way, and you can save your river power for showing others how much you care.

No matter whether your style is volcano, iceberg, rock, or river, you have some control over how you react. The next time the room heats up with an argument, think about being a lake—cool, calm, and deep.

alike or different?

Figuring out how you are similar to and different from the people in your family can help you understand them—and understand how to get along with them. Maybe you have a quick temper, but your sister rarely gets upset. Maybe you and your grandpa both giggle when you're nervous. Think about it!

Ready for a challenge? On the next two pages, write down the names of three people in your family.

Get set. Find a timer and set it for three minutes. During those three minutes, think of all the ways you are similar to and different from the people you chose. You don't need to write full sentences. Just jot down enough to make the idea clear. You can write about physical attributes (you both have green eyes), artistic tastes (neither of you likes opera), or emotional things (you both cry at movies or yell when you're mad).

Go! Start the timer.

Name: _____

How we're alike: _____

_____

_____

How we're different: _____

_____

_____

Name: _____

How we're alike: _____

_____

_____

How we're different: _____

_____

_____

Name: _____

How we're alike: _____

_____

_____

How we're different: _____

_____

_____

When three minutes are up, stop and count your answers. Whose "alike" list is the longest? Whose "different" list is the longest?

The person most like you may be the one you get along with best. The person most different from you may be someone you have trouble understanding sometimes. Getting along with that person may require your best negotiating skills as you state your opinions. Either way, you can learn from your lists!

word power

Words are powerful things, whether you're working things out with a parent, stepparent, brother, sister, stepsibling, or naughty dog. Say the words below out loud. Pause after each word to notice how it makes your body feel.

Chances are, saying these words made you feel something. The kinder words—sweetie, love, and honey—may have given you a little smile inside or made you feel positive. The unkind words—klutz, stupid, worthless, and loser—may have made you utter a mental "ouch."

Just as these words made you feel good or bad, the words you use affect the emotions of everyone in your family. When you say loving words or fighting ones, the emotional temperature at your house changes instantly!

translation, please

Angry words often mean more than one thing and can stem from more than one feeling. The words below are good examples. Draw lines from the sentences on the left to their most likely meanings on the right. Then look at the red words to see what feelings might cause someone to burst out with these phrases.

Words

Meanings

1. You're not the boss of me!

2. You lied to me!

3. Shut up!

4. You're stupid!

a. Something changed, and I don't like it!
CONFUSED
DISAPPOINTED

b. I can't deal with this right now. Leave me alone.
STRESSED OUT
ASHAMED

c. I feel so bad about myself that I have to tell you you're no good, too.
AFRAID

d. I'm not in control.
HELPLESS
POWERLESS

ANSWERS: 1 matches best with d, 2 matches best with a, 3 matches best with b, and 4 matches best with c.

BIG truth

Your words have power. Use them for good.

neutral words

A fight is like a fire, and neutral words are like water—they make the fire go out. The next time you're in a heated argument, try using some of these peacemaking phrases. They don't mean that you agree or give in, but they will cool things down.

Let me think about that.

I know we both want to work this out.

You have a point.

I hear what you're saying.

Hmmm . . .

You have a point.

Wait . . . What? Really?

talking it out

Try these conversation starters when you want to come to an understanding with someone.

I'm ready to make peace. Are you?

I don't like it when we fight.

I feel sad that we argued. Can we try that again?

Read body language. You may not need to say anything to get a conversation rolling. Look into the other person's eyes. If you see love there, you can offer a hug. Chances are that will naturally get the talk flowing!

Brainstorm. Ask the other person to brainstorm with you about some ways you can avoid having the same quarrel again. Two brains are better than one—at least they are when they're not in an argument!

I have a sister who is five years old. If we get into a fight and I want to make up, I offer to play with her. She loves that.

—Skylar, age 10

let's make a deal

You may not realize that you already know how to negotiate. But you do. Whether you're the oldest child, an only child, the youngest in the family, or anywhere in between, you work out agreements with family members all the time.

Think about the past few days. What deals did you make with people in your family? Did everybody get what they wanted? Did you have any arguments that could have been solved through negotiation? List a few examples of these deals and arguments here.

Deals I made:

_____

_____

_____

_____

Arguments that could have been deals:

_____

_____

_____

_____

I don't have to use the computer right now, but I really need it after dinner.

If we make a schedule for sharing the bedroom, we can both have private time.

I'll vacuum the living room if you'll take out the garbage.

chilling out

Have you ever noticed how bad your body feels after an argument? Being in a fight robs you of energy and peace. So take care of yourself. Try the following ideas for chilling out when family fever runs high.

Just breathe. Deep breathing will soothe and steady you. If someone says something that gets you riled, before you say anything back, take two breaths. Breathe in through your nose and out through your mouth. This alone can take the wind out of an argument.

l..o..n..g, s..l..o..w

Understand that you're mad all over. Getting angry affects more than your heart and your head. Your whole body feels it! When you're angry, your heart beats faster, your muscles tense, your breathing speeds up, and your brain produces "angry" chemicals. It can take at least 20 minutes for all of that to go away. Until then, some part of your body is still mad! Give yourself time to calm down.

Calm down by getting physical. Can't stop an argument? Say, "You know, I'm feeling _____," and fill in the emotion you feel. Then explain: "I need time to calm down." Leave the scene, and get moving! Shoot hoops, go for a walk or a run, ride your bike, or climb a tree. Use your muscles to calm your mind.

Ask questions. When you feel calmer, ask yourself some questions about what happened. This gets the thinking part of your brain working rather than the feelings part. Writing your answers in a journal may help you think more clearly.

Have some gumption. If you argue with someone you love, odds are you'll feel pretty awful about it. But part of living in a family is learning to stand up for yourself. If your brother teases you too harshly, say so. If you got blamed for something that you didn't do, say so.

You don't have to yell to do this. You just have to keep saying how you feel and what you need until somebody hears you! If things get tense, be patient and keep talking. This is what it means to stand on your own two feet.

your personal first-aid kit

Some families have quiet disagreements; others have big, loud clashes. Big or little, family conflicts can make our hearts hurt. Put a check mark next to the ideas you can use to take care of yourself when there is tension in your family. Add your own ideas in the blank spaces.

I can . . .

☐ remind myself that even when we argue, we still love one another.

☐ cry and let my feelings out.

☐ ask for a comforting hug.

☐ move my body and get physical.

☐ talk to a good friend about my feelings.

☐ ask for help from a loving adult.

☐ write or draw how I feel.

☐ go outside and soak up some nature.

☐ _____

☐ _____

☐ _____

saying "sorry"

If you did something that hurt someone's feelings, you need to try to make things right. Apologizing will help you—and the other person— feel better, and then you can start fresh.

Keep the apology short and simple. Just say you're sorry for what you did or said. Resist the urge to make excuses or explain why you did what you did. That way, the apology won't be about YOU but about the person who was hurt.

About that lump in your throat: Sometimes apologizing can be embarrassing, even painful. If you need courage, give yourself a little time—but don't avoid apologizing.

GET CLOSE . . . AND CLOSER!

The secret to getting closer to your family
is being curious about their stories, their dreams,
and their hearts. Have fun together! Here are some
activities you can do that will make you smile—and
help you get to know one another even better.

family fun facts

How well do you know your family? Complete the sentences below by circling a family member and filling in the blank. Next, become a reporter. Interview your family members to see how many of the questions you answered right.

1. One of my mom's/dad's favorite books is
_____.

2. My sister's/brother's favorite room in our house is
_____.

3. One of my mom's/dad's favorite movies is
_____.

4. When my grandmother/grandfather was a child, she/he lived in
_____.

5. When my other grandmother/grandfather was a child,
she/he lived in _____.

6. At my age, my mom/dad wanted to be a
_____ when she/he grew up.

7. If my brother/sister could travel anywhere in the world, it
would be _____.

8. One of the biggest adventures my mom/dad ever had was
_____.

9. One of my mom's/dad's closest friends is named
_____.

10. My sister's/brother's best part of the day is
_____.

11. My mom's/dad's favorite kind of music is
_____.

Scoring

9 or more correct
Congratulations! You listen closely to the people in your family. If knowing fun facts about your family were a contest, you'd win first prize!

5–8 correct
You've been doing a good job paying attention to details in your family. With a little work, you'll know all your family trivia!

4 or fewer correct
There's a whole world of fun family facts out there to discover. The more you know about your family members, the better you'll understand them—and that can mean more closeness and good times at home.

Celebrate your specialness! Every family member has quirks. Strange as it sounds, those are things that can make families closer.

My dad is a terrible singer. When he sings, my sister and I start singing as loud as we can so we can't hear him, but then he sings louder. Then my mom starts yelling at us all to be quiet. The weird thing is we do this every day!
—Madeline, age 11

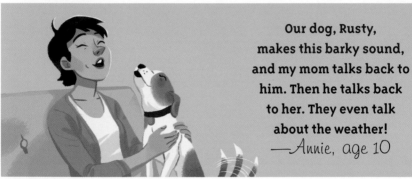

Our dog, Rusty, makes this barky sound, and my mom talks back to him. Then he talks back to her. They even talk about the weather!
—Annie, age 10

My mom gets excited over nothing. Today she started dancing because she got a book about flowers. It was crazy.
—Kellye, age 12

cute! cute! cute!

My aunt always says, "Cute, cute, cute!" when she likes something. She says it three times, never once or twice—always three.
—Rhonda, age 11

Enjoy the nighttime neighborhood. If you live in a place where you can walk at night, ask your family to take an evening stroll. The world feels totally different in the dark, and there's a special closeness that comes from seeing your street at bedtime. Besides, a walk in the evening is a good time for sharing stories of the day or memories from the past. Don't forget a flashlight!

Share your dreams. When you wake up, tell the story of your dream to a parent or sibling quickly, before you forget. Does anybody in your family have ideas about what your dream might mean? Are there clues in the dream that can help you solve a daytime problem? If morning is too busy, write down your dream and share it in the evening. Ask your family what they dreamed about, too!

Join family members while they do something they love. Watch hockey with your brother, or listen to jazz with your mom. Make dinner or hit golf balls with your dad. Even if it's not your favorite thing to do, it will draw you closer. Maybe next time, they'll do what you love to do—with you!

Play "Best Thing, Worst Thing." At the dinner table, ask each person to tell the best thing that happened that day. Then ask each person to tell the worst part of his or her day. If people are in a joking mood, have a contest to see who had the very best and very worst days. If your family is feeling serious, simply share your stories. Either way, you'll feel closer than you did before!

Get game crazy. Talk with your family about regularly setting aside an evening to play games. You could call it Find Family Fun Night! On FFF Night, turn off computers, the TV, and phones, and break out a game. Teach a younger sibling how to play something new. Other times, choose a game based on luck so that even little sibs will have a chance to win.

Play by the numbers. Grab any family member, or divide your family into two teams. Write the list below on another sheet of paper so that you have two copies. Yell "One, two, three—go!" and see which team can find the answers most quickly.

When you're done, see if both teams got the same answers. The team with the most correct answers gets to take the other team out for ice cream!

Number of jars of peanut butter in the house

Number of windows in the house

Number of pets in the family

Number of shoes in the front closet

Number of steps leading up to the front door

Number of chairs at the dinner table

Number of sinks in the house

Number of lights in the living room

Number of pillows in the house

Number of phones the family has

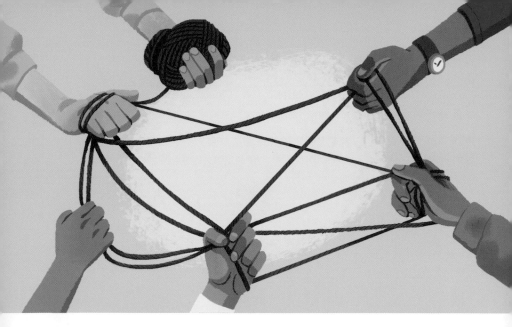

Get tangled up in love. Find a ball of yarn or string. Ask your family to stand in a circle. Start by holding the end of the string and tossing the ball to someone else. (It will unwind as you toss it.) After you toss the ball, say something good about the person who caught it.

Next, have the catcher toss the ball to someone else—still holding on to part of the string—and say what he or she appreciates about that person. Keep tossing the ball around the circle until the string is all unwound. What a web of good feelings you made!

Plant memories. Plant a tree or a bush together to mark a family event. Graduating from elementary school? That's a big event. Anniversaries and birthdays are, too. So are sad times such as losing a grandparent. Your family will feel connected on the day you plant the tree and when you see it throughout the year.

Send signals. Speak your own private language by making up family-only code words or signals. A tug on your ear could mean "Look at that." Saying "FHB" when guests are over for dinner could be code for "family, hold back" so that there will be plenty of food for guests. But be careful about using family signals in public. They can give you incurable giggles!

If something comes up at dinner that my mom doesn't want me to hear, she says, "Come help me with the dishes." Everybody laughs because we all know what she means!
—Victoria, age 10

Once we were at the zoo and couldn't find the bathroom. We also couldn't find the elephants. So now when we say, "Where is the elephant?" it really means something else!
—Fran, age 9

Make it official. Schools have official songs. States have official birds. Why not your family? Brainstorm with other family members to fill in the blanks below:

Family song: _____

Family mascot: _____

Family food: _____

Family cheer: _____

_____

_____

Family color: _____

Family bird: _____

Draw your family flag here.
(Include symbols, words, and colors that represent your family to you.)

Look into the future. Make a list of things that are true right now about you and your family. You can also make predictions for the coming year. Seal the list in an envelope marked "Open Next Year." Pack it away with the holiday decorations. Read the list together next year to see how things have changed!

Share a read. Have you read a good book recently? Your family might enjoy lots of the books you like, too. Loan a book to your mom, dad, sister, or brother. Talk about the plot twists, and compare what you thought. ("Could you believe the ending?" "What would you have done in her place?" "I cried in that part, too.")

Cheer for the home team. What are the biggest challenges your family members are going through? Is your brother having a hard time with math? Has your mom been spending long hours working? Leave a note cheering him or her on. Knowing that you believe in them will help your family members face their troubles and reach their goals.

Do you have a family tale to tell?

Write to us!
Understanding Families Editor
American Girl
8400 Fairway Place
Middleton, WI 53562

Here are some other American Girl books you might like:

Each sold separately. Find more books online at americangirl.com.

family fun coupons and awards

Use these handy pullouts to show your family that you
appreciate them, when you need help apologizing,
or when you just want to say thanks.

FAMILY AWARD

This award goes to

_____

for being by far the most stupendous and wonderful

_____

in the family, in the whole world, and
possibly in the entire universe.

From: _____

FAMILY AWARD

This award goes to

_____

for being by far the most stupendous and wonderful

_____

in the family, in the whole world, and
possibly in the entire universe.

From: _____

Official "I'm Sorry" Certificate
from the Department of Apologies and Mended Fences

To: _____

I am genuinely sorry for what I did. I know it made you feel

- ☐ sad
- ☐ angry
- ☐ upset
- ☐ all of the above

I care about you very much. Please accept my apology.

From: _____

©/TM 2019 American Girl

Official "I'm Sorry" Certificate
from the Department of Apologies and Mended Fences

To: _____

I am genuinely sorry for what I did. I know it made you feel

- ☐ sad
- ☐ angry
- ☐ upset
- ☐ all of the above

I care about you very much. Please accept my apology.

From: _____

©/TM 2019 American Girl

Official "I'm Sorry" Certificate
from the Department of Apologies and Mended Fences

To: _____

I am genuinely sorry for what I did. I know it made you feel

- ☐ sad
- ☐ angry
- ☐ upset
- ☐ all of the above

I care about you very much. Please accept my apology.

From: _____

©/TM 2019 American Girl

The Chore Store Gift Card

One chore done by me
when YOU want it done
with **no complaining**

To: _____

From: _____

Date: _____

1 free smile included

The Chore Store Gift Card

One chore done by me
when YOU want it done
with **no complaining**

To: _____

From: _____

Date: _____

1 free smile included

The Chore Store Gift Card

One chore done by me
when YOU want it done
with **no complaining**

To: _____

From: _____

Date: _____

1 free smile included

Official Note of Thanks

from the Department of Good Manners and Appreciation

Dear _____

I would like to thank you for _____

_____

It means a lot to me because _____

_____

It was nice of you to do what you did. So thanks, thanks,
and more thanks, from the bottom of my heart.

From: _____

Official Note of Thanks

from the Department of Good Manners and Appreciation

Dear _____

I would like to thank you for _____

_____

It means a lot to me because _____

_____

It was nice of you to do what you did. So thanks, thanks,
and more thanks, from the bottom of my heart.

From: _____

Official Note of Thanks
from the Department of Good Manners and Appreciation

Dear _____

I would like to thank you for _____

_____

It means a lot to me because _____

_____

It was nice of you to do what you did. So thanks, thanks,
and more thanks, from the bottom of my heart.

From: _____

©/TM 2019 American Girl

Official Note of Thanks
from the Department of Good Manners and Appreciation

Dear _____

I would like to thank you for _____

_____

It means a lot to me because _____

_____

It was nice of you to do what you did. So thanks, thanks,
and more thanks, from the bottom of my heart.

From: _____

©/TM 2019 American Girl